Anhedonia Delirium

Courtney Whitaker

BookLeaf Publishing

India | USA | UK

Anhedonia Delirium © 2023 Courtney Whitaker

All rights reserved.

No part of this publication may be reproduced, stored in a retrieval system, or transmitted, in any form or by any means, electronic, mechanical, photocopying, recording or otherwise, without the prior written permission of the presenters.

Courtney Whitaker asserts the moral right to be identified as author of this work.

Presentation by *BookLeaf Publishing*

Web: www.bookleafpub.com

E-mail: info@bookleafpub.com

ISBN: 9789358737622

First edition 2023

Broken AC in July

Don't look for me now
I don't want to be found
I'm dissociating in the tub
The water - louche
A lukewarm absinthe, anxious
I'm not sure I can still hold me
Together, sugar cube that I am
Flames licking me up
On a silver spoon
Though it's not really a
Choice I get to make
I have no room for self-indulgent
Self-pity
I'm mother to two little dragons
I have mouths to feed

I have souls to nourish
So I will have to melt slowly
Into this drink, this tub
Keeping me a little cool
In the unbearable heat
Of a house that is broken
And I have not yet recovered
From a friend's recent suicide
Cruel and ugly -

Plagiarisms and platitudes
So raw with disbelief and muddy grief
I water the world on fire
Hoping for relief
But the AC is broken
A perpetual onslaught

Of unfortunate things
It reminds me of being a kid
Trying to sleep in the Atlanta heat
As I feverishly fantasized
Cool air and hot water
I can survive all of this
I will always be ok
A remarkable heart I possess
Raging against roaring winds
It's only that sometimes I
Can't be reached - I have to cut
Off my own head
And float for a while

Witch

Her veil envelops me
Deep amber, smell of metallic earth
Scraped through teeth
Her warm shadow my bed
Venus in slurs
I sleep with her name
On my breath
I find her keys everywhere -
In my coffee, on the floor
In my hair
And once, behind my eye
Like a lost contact
I am claimed and protected
Enmeshed with Goddess burnished bronze

Under cool fingers on my burning cheek I find a
strength
Not native to my cells
An awakening not consented to
However necessary - I, delicate
Daughter, wear her echoes as
Earrings
Walk the earth with a name
Both revered and reviled
Witch

I have an army of angry ghosts
Slap scattered across my aura
A threatening pulse
Behind my darling smile

Sick in October

Lying ill, a white sheet
Thrown on the floor
The door is open and
The October air feels like a
Promise
I have strings of pearls around my
Neck
I have claustrophobic decadence
I red lipped grimace and a failed attempt
To alchemize my shortness of breath
Into a fetish
I am sick in October and dismayed
In isolation
I feel like a dangerous thing
I am ill and wheezing and ohhh so
Delicately feminine. Demure
Disease
I am a vector
Singing silence, I marvel at the mist
From my throat
I push plague from my lungs
I have always been drowning
But to breach the surface, this is
A startling cruelty, to catch
Your breath

To be held above the waves
Only to slip back under
It's warm in October and
The silky air dances over
My vulnerability
A dress of nothingness

Try Harder to be Softer

The harder you grip me
The quicker I slip
From your hands
Slip slide right out
And away from you
I am not
Able to be held
By a show of strength
Rather
You must try harder
To be softer
To be kind at your core
To have a head-tilting
Perspective
Or something that

Fascinates, something weird
Something that's
Mysterious
To glue me
To you

Hungry for Hell

One small misstep
Is all it would take
For me to trip
And tumble down
Gown billowing
Hair twisting
Mouth open, shocked
Down the black tunnel
To be caught
By two strong arms
Pinned
And before I can catch
My breath
Or stand up
I know
My breath
Or stand up
I know

In my heart of hearts
That this is my home, this
Underworld
And I don't want to be
Not caught
By the king

Of my heated heart
Six little seeds
Tie me home
I wish to eat the entire
Ruby-red bloody sweet
Pomegranate
Ensnare me, I am
Rewilded
I am hungry for Hell

I am hungry for
The seeds in the palm
Of his hand

Unstitched

We stitched ourselves together
Conjoined twins
Of our own device
Some stitches sewn with love
Others, trauma
Our hearts gravitated to where
We did our work
And they were stitched together, too
We were left and right
We were so similar that our parents
Couldn't tell us apart
When we grew it hurt
The stitches pulled tight
Popping, bleeding
And one of us began to cut the threads
one of us
And then the other
Secretly disengaging
We noticed we were loose
At the ankles
We could move more freely
Our calves came undone, then
Our thighs, our hips
We let the little holes heal
When we got further up, rib cage

Our sewn together hearts
It was an agony
It couldn't happen all at once
Fatal if done too quickly
One by one the stitches popped
A violent undoing
A violent undoing
An unstitching
I barely survived
I'll never sew the stitches again
I couldn't do it
Again

The Persistence of Ghosts

Sometimes in the morning
When I'm cooking alone
And its quiet
I hear my long-gone friend
"Stir it like you love it"
Gorgeous girl, vibrant laughing
Dead for years
And sometimes in the evening
When I'm reading
And its quiet
I hear a ghost say
"You're going to love this one" handing me a
book
Black glasses slipping down his nose
Hair askew
And sometimes when I get dressed
And its quiet
I hear her say, eyes narrowed
"Your blacks don't match"
And I think I don't care
I'm not the matchy-matchy type
But I still change
My shirt
And these ghosts persist
I wonder if I'll always hear them

In the silences
Of my aliveness
13

Anhedonia Delirium

There is no antidote for my
Anhedonia
I taste nothing
There is no cure
For this malady
No remedy
For feeling nothing at all
I am more afraid
Of this living death
Than dying
I deny all signs
Of an incoming
Anhedonia delirium
Trying this medicine, running
Fighting

But every time it comes
Unstoppable
Ruthless
A wave overcomes me
And I exist underwater
Until a kind tide
Throws me back on shore
Half-drowned and savage
Feral mermaid

Feeling all the broken glass
Under my feet
The glorious sensation
Evoking tears of joy
On my blank space
Of a face

Metamorphosis

An ecstasy
Obliterating
This place
This cocoon - this repulsive
Insect cave
A suffocating wrapping
Of our own creation
It is a home of agony
It is all our bones
Breaking
It is a melting away
Of the flesh we thought
Was home
This chrysalis - a place of pain and yes
We emerge more
Beautiful, changed
An evolution forged
In misery

Psychopomp Paramour

I was yours for just a little while
While you needed me I was yours and it was
good
To stretch to your needs, to contort to your
moods
It was an interesting exercise in getting
Bent out of shape while not getting bent
Out of shape. I learned to sit in silence
I learned to be still, to be a face in the window
Waiting for you to come back
A loving, languishing body in the bed
You made me into a doll, and you played
Tea with me, pouring me hot cups of coffee and
speaking
into my button-eyes, my mouth not moving but
you hear
All the words you want to hear
Until I shake at the panic you fill me with and
you get a glimpse
Of the human-flesh beneath the porcelain.
The moments you hurt me were the only ones
In which you glimpsed my aliveness.
I was yours for just a little while
Between the worlds, delivering you from one
side

To the other, an intense and blank presence
Screaming you are not alone, but you can't hear
My doll's cries. I am not really real for you.
In the swallowing dark you found me.
But even dolls get lost
When men handle them too rough.

Just You

I have tried to distract myself
I have grown gardens and forged alliances
With deadly dangerous and wild stalking puma
I have eaten entire countries
Swallowed oceans, slept 1,000 years
I have tried to forget the timbre of your voice
By slicing off my ears with a second-hand
scimitar
Smothering myself under the pillows you slept
on
I don't want to feel you in my head anymore
Autodefenestration
The immortal heart ties itself to the tracks
And relishes the squeal of the train
Such a mess
I have tried to distract myself
And it's not working, not when every breath
rhymes
With your name

Love You Like Lemons

I love you like
Lemons in December
And perfect pink flowers
Blooming in the chill
I love you so much
My ribs can't contain it
And it bursts out of me
Like fat fuzzy bees
Swarming the garden
I love you like sugar
Slowly stirred, dissolving
In your favorite drink
I'm sure my love for you
Is a sticky contagion -
That the whole world
Will be infected and
No one will be able to help
But to love you, too

Asinine thoughts on Asthma

Each breath I take is a gift
I lift the corners of my heart
To find what's there - is it air?
While you think about pretty shapes
Heart shapes, love shapes, I am imagining
Two lungs crushed like flowers
In a heavy book

Every turn around the corner is a precipice
I am at risk of drowning anytime
What will find me today?
Inhale, constrict, inflict a sudden panic
Bright as an orange flame
In the cage in my chest.

I will be pressed
To death. Witch. Piling heavy stones
One on top of the next
Giles Corey is my patron saint
See me through this crushing
Rush of air out, no way back in
Saint Giles, curl your hand to mine

Can you, can anyone, breathe
For me?

Can you suck the air from out there
And put it in my waiting, deflated
Sense of lungspace?

A Dirge for my Dresses

Looking through the closet
Through the dark doors
The clinking of hangers
Bumping elbows as I
Push through the fabrics with my fingers
Looking with the feel of
Cotton, silk, and some other
Shiny texture, a floral print
A bloody red, a boho shift
Shifts, shivers, falls
I have this collection
Of dresses I can't wear
Because they all bear
Some memory of you
Touching them, too
And sometimes I fantasize
A conflagration of gowns
A bright, blazing bonfire
To cleanse my closet
What then
Should I pull over my
Singed skin
Will I be able to shroud
My body
In foggy fabrics

Will they erase the face
that looked into mine
As I wore this dress
Or that dress to see you
To see me.

Ouiji

25

In exchange for a soft white bite
Into my throat I'm gifted shiny trinkets
They appear in a glass bowl, iridescent, I don't
remember buying it,
I put it by my ouija board
Sometimes the blood has dried to the sheet
I have to tear the sticky fabric
From my neck
He keeps reopening the same wound
I'm feeling ecstatic, anemic,
I know I didn't dream it, my planchette jerking
to each letter, he spells
"EYELOVEYOUEYELOVEYOU"
And I know what he means

Himlock

He pours the tea, he says
"I have added one little drop
Of poison. It's a big glass.
It's only one little drop of poison.
Will you still drink it?"
I say "no," then I take a long,
Delicious, deliberate sip
Of his tea
And he promises to hurt me
I say, yes, as if he needs
My consent, rather he craves
My encouragement
Yes, yes, yes, it's ok
It hurts like the sun shining
On the darkest parts of me
It's an agony, a kiss with teeth

Floranym

In the mirror, roses
I glimpse my reddest raw
Petal soft
The illusory invitation
I am the heady, floral perfume
You can't get out of your clothes
The sweetest scent, strangling
This face, smiling, these arms
Stiff leaves, leaving you
Wondering
Why I grow best with roots
Soaked in blood, why the sun
Withers me, delicate in my
Violence
Venus adores me
Violence
Named for an ancestor
I don't remember
Marked at birth
For gorgeous danger
A tradition I continued
Before
My tower year
My penance is her
Wildness, my spring - off

A yet unidentified species
Of rose
Burdened with femaleness
But left to scream, loud as red

Premonitions

I had this dream
With hanging upside down bats
And alligators waiting
To be fed behind uncertain
Barriers
And I had money in my
Wallet when I looked again
And I had honey in my
Words when I spoke again
And I was falling through water
And I couldn't see a face but I felt
A presence
Something is coming, something warm
A place to fall
Something will happen
Before the summer ends
I feel the shift
In my world, in my gut
And I'm opening up
My hands are stretched out, up
Waiting for it to fall to me.

Always

White feathers line the spot where I
Fell from the sky, my team of spirits
Worked diligently to ghost pad the ground
And while startled, I landed in love
I am Divinely Protected
My corporeal body a beautiful distraction
Your jealous eyes have no effect
This little bird keeps her heart open
Her soul at her fingertips
I forgive their missteps, their harm
I feel so sad for those who hurt and try to hurt
and succeed to hurt
Me. I stay soft, I stay wild.
I am the child of a child and a child

www.ingramcontent.com/pod-product-compliance
Lightning Source LLC
Chambersburg PA
CBHW071241140726
47996CB00007B/2711